Tell The Bees

a collection of love and lust poems

by Annette Marie Smith

First Printing: 2015

ISBN: 978-0692581162

Lucky Horseshoe Publishing
2285 University Ave. W.
Saint Paul, MN 55114

www.annettemariesmith.com

I have lips the size of violets
not lotus lush or rose blown
but shaped to desire anyway,
lips that take small sips
and me like a hummingbird
hovering over
the nectar of you.
– AMS

Contents

Acknowledgements

Special thanks to the following publications where these pieces first appeared:
Twilight Times ~ “Day Longs for Night”
Poems Niederngasse ~ “A Fairy Tale Come True”
Newspaper Tree ~ “With Birds”
Empowerment4Women Magazine ~ “Winter Things”
Fables ~ “The Golden Bough”

I want to eat poetry like honey

right off the comb
and dripping deliciously
for another's tongue to dip in as well –
honey for two with the feel of wild words
still buzzing
and the smell of clover and lilacs, roses and sweetsuckle
but also containing the dizzy rocking of rope ladders
used to reach the impossible heights
of Himalayan mountain honey caves
and rhododendron sighs.

Intimate Terms

I am on intimate terms with the cold
its hard mouth at my breast
its fingers crackling through my hair
my knees so giddy they can't keep still.
All of these things,
the tightening, the shaking, the mussed up hair
would be something desired
were cold replaced with you.

I chiseled you from dreams

the marble of your integrity
hard beneath my hands
the gold veins of your allure
open
and getting in my hair.
I reached
calloused fingers
across time and desire
and found you deifying there
beautiful to me even with my eyes closed.
Not just the thorn and petal
but the very root of my heart's rose.

Full Cold Moon

She is fat with the satisfaction of her cold light.
She is fecund with frosty happiness.
The clouds are slips of lace, mere lingerie,
and the night watches transfixed as she lets them drift away.
She pulls the night in closer,
as if he is the tide at her command.
And in a way he is, this lover of hers
who is always with her —
and stirs her darker side.
The moan that she rouses in him
is the true origin
of the first wolf's howl
and in this way too they are always paired.
Longing made manifest
in the soul song of one of earth's best creatures
is their gift to each other–
that and their child
that they both dote on
known as Lunacy.
The light and the dark and the passion make
a beautiful sorcery.

Fitted Shirt and Flowers in His Beard

(after Short Skirt/Long Jacket by Cake)

I want a man with a fitted shirt and flowers in his beard.
I want a man with a rough road and the means to take me there.
We will meet on a trail through the woods when we bump into each other
because we were both busy looking up at the sky.
I want a man who knows where he's going
with a pen in his hand and the right way of holding it.
He will tilt the world just a bit with the way that he smiles.
I want a man with eyes like pages I can get lost in.
He is pouring his voice out like rain mixed with honey.
He is carrying something with strength and with gentleness.
The fit of his compassion makes me feel shy.
I want a man with a fitted shirt and flowers in his beard.

Your Hands

Your hands are books full of wonder
leaning on the shelf of my hips.
I want you
to open your books and give me a lesson.

Ama

I would dive, let my fingertips become hard,
calloused, and markedly round.
I would clench a knife with my teeth.
I would tremble in the depths and leave
even the memory of breath
behind on the beach
smothered in sand and out of reach.
I would gather, softly, softly,
shimmering abalone and curling seaweed —
all for your pearls if your pearls were for me.

There is magic

in the air
slanting down in moonbeams
like Cupid's arrows
penning love songs to the night.
You are also an arrow
in the night, a shot with aim that's true.
I feel you
spinning your magic like motorcycle wheels
right outside my window
and from five floors up
I reach out and catch some
moonbeams
some magic
and a tiny smudge of you
in my hands like I am a heroine
who catches fletched arrows in her hand
and I tuck that arrow behind my ear
like a pencil.
I will use it to write my answer
and then I will pull the bowstring of my heart
and shoot it back to you.

"Do You Want To Watch The Fireworks With Me?" He Texts

And at first glance I think he has asked me to watch
firewords with him
and a great excitement seizes me
as I imagine what that will entail
but then I see that he has asked me
to watch the holiday weekend fireworks with him.
"Haha!" I tell him, "I thought you wanted me to see
'firewords' with you!"
And he says "I do.
I want to paint words for you with the fire of my desire
the burst of my longing visible far and wide
in the night sky
my feelings for you flowering in fireworks
that look like rockets to others while you and I both know
they are pyrotechnics launched by you."
Well, yes. I would like to see his fireworks.

Poème 31

My lashes sweep down
a symphony of violin bows
strung with pieces of night
instead of mare hair.
My mouth is a bow too
but of a more martial kind
lacquered
a red as dark as chocolate
with arrowhead kisses
dipped in Farenfew wine.
My pulse points are drums dressed
in thin skins of parfumé
they beat like moths
drawn to pheromone flame
and the song of the night swells up all around me
in the strains of the violin rain.

Tempest, Whirlwind, Blizzard

She is a storm
and the only way to weather her
is to take her in your arms
embrace the wildness
and dance.

He ate their love

from the inside out
as if he were a green worm
(a green worm with a myriad feet)
endlessly dissatisfied
never satiated
in the very heart
of the red and shiny apple
that was oh so delicious
but only after it was all
completely gone.
And that is when he found out too
that there never was any such thing
as a core.
He ate that apple up
from stem to bottom
through and through.
She named him jealousy.
But his teeth -- more numerous even
than his caterpillar creeping feet --
were made of envy too.

The Night Is an Aerial Silk Performer

I see the way the night kisses you –
all down the length of you her kisses wind
along the ropes of your muscles.
She is performing an aerial routine
and you are the scarves holding her up.
She momentarily stops at the top of your clavicle
to remove your shirt with her teeth like stars
that sparkle lark song
and then she starts again
from the other side.
She rides the silk of your cords and lingers leaving
you half in shadow
as she licks and tastes herself on your skin,
breathes in the smell of leather and woodland moss,
and she, like me,
pleasures in finding something of her own
wildness in the smell of you.
She wraps herself up in you like she belongs there,
the night, but she leaves room for me.

Ever since Persephone

raised the pulp of pomegranate to her mouth
touched the redness of that fruit to her own lips
(incidentally inventing lipstick)
and gave herself –
with hell to pay (wink) –
to the pleasure of abandoning restraint
in the teeth of the moment,
ever since then her descendants
in spirit
have also savored the pomegranate –
a grenade the color of passion
with seeds that teem with risque.

Riddle Poem #5

I'll give your feet wings.
I'll put the wind in your hair
as you grab handfuls of sunshine
and walk on the air.

I'll take your composure.
I'll make your breath bolt
like a frightened rabbit
down its deep holt.

I burn and I sear.
I flicker and flash.
I can be resurrected
from embers and ash.

I can blind you
and dazzle you.
I have a real flair.
I am, as they say,
a true ____ ______.

Two words, what am I?
Love affair.

Come to Me, Spring

I will wear you like a dress.
I will sway to your briers and birdsong,
twirl as you flare out spinning
with giddy color and scent and sound
and I will look
for the one that is worthy
to see this embroidered profusion
caressing the curves of me
these sap filled, honey filled, days.
And I will find the one deserving
to pick the flowers from this dress
and gather them into bouquets
as the green-green and the shimmer –
of lepidoptera wings, of delicate scales,
and ribbons of feathers –
pools at my mud kissed feet.

The Better To

"Danger's teeth are footstools for my feet", she said.
The wolf looked down and saw that her shoes were very
pointy indeed.
He also noted, with his sensitive ears, the clink of steel
beneath her skirts.
Did she wear a belly chain strung with knives instead of
charms?
Was that a trap made of the things that all wolves fear
dangling like an evening bag from her wrist?
His tender foot pads clenched in its imagined grip.
Her charms and traps had teeth sharper than his own.
"AOOUUUUUUUUUUUUUUUUUUU! YIP! YIP!" the wolf
said.
He met her eyes and saw that she was smiling.
Should he follow her to "Grandma's" house
or just gnaw off his foot right here?

Crackling Crown
(from the Night Fairytales series)

In the fall, when I let you go
and this was just before the snow
nothing remained of you or your touch.
Only the leaves, where we lay down
only the leaves, clung to my hair
a crackling crown of memories.

Let March Be My Missive
(after Pablo Neruda's "Every Day You Play", 1924)

I want to do with you
what spring does
to the waters pent
in pristine prisons.

Sparks

I can hear your breath creak
stretched thin on the scrubbing board of the air.
Your glance is static electricity.
Your hands are heat's secret lair.
I don't waste my breath on punitive air.
I spark my glance against yours.
And my hands too
are a place where heat burrows.
Let me show that nest to you.

Firelight

Your scent stays with me
like wood smoke on this cold night
reminding me of fire
and the way that I caution myself
as I inch closer and closer to you
that fire is beautiful
but it also burns.
Long after I am in bed
under the covers
and surrounded by pillows
my dreaming self reaches out
drawn to the warmth of your flame.
I wake with roses trellising my cheeks
like a crop of kisses.
I warm my cold fingers
and cool my hot cheeks
one with the other
while firelight dances
with thoughts of you
in the room behind my closed eyes.

I Hope You Do Something Nice

I hope you do something nice
With that piece of my heart I gave you.
Use it like a match
To strike a smile
To light a fire some cold day to keep you warm.

Hang it like a painting on your most desolate wall.
There will be a shaft of sunlight that plays across its surface
Acting like a prism and throwing refracted light
Around that painting on your wall.
Let the colors dance.

Hold it between your hands
Like a mug of hot cocoa
With whipped cream
Topped with stiff peaks.
Lick your lips and sip
On memories of me.

Use it as a paperweight
On the desk of your regard for me
Something with gravitas
To pin the rustling notes of your affections
In one place.

Carry it in your pocket like a good luck charm.
When your spirit is low
Rub it till it shines and think of me.
I will come to you like a genie summoned from her lamp
Whether it be in a phone call, text, or dream.

I will come to you because you have a part of me.

Dreamcatcher

The night is a sieve that can't hold all
the dreams I keep dreaming of you.
I need a net of moonbeams and sighs
with starlight that twinkles on its handle that shines
like a wand that grants wishes and dowses desires.
If granted this power of midnight runed wood
I promise to use it only for good.

Last night I tucked my head under the blankets of night,

black and embroidered bright with stars.
The moonlight curled like a white cat
purring at my feet
while I stayed up late to read the story of you.
The wind sighed through the branches
and made me shiver to recall
the whisper of your voice
against my hair
and winding through the chambers of my ear.
Your breath carried keys and opened up doors
that made me wish and want and need
to listen to so much more.
So, sign the guest book of my mind.
You spent the night in my dreams.

Sunrise

"I want to put the sun in the sky for you," he said
"I want to light up your world."
But she already had her hands full of sunshine as it was
and just wanted him
to help her hold it
as she hoisted the sun into the sky.

She wanted to turn the world on together.
Or at least take turns lighting it for each other.

She plays the part of wicked queen

(from the Night Fairytales series)

asking you to bring her own heart to her
like Snow White's stepmother grim
against herself.

You take the huntsman's role and you begin
by saying, "I have it right here
it beats like a bird
in its tree made into box,"

and looking in for her wild heart
she sees your own within.

A Long Monsoon of You

You are a rain song
caressing turrets, tiles, and cobblestones.
Your words are water kicking up its heels
against the slanted roofs of my ears.
You fill the deep wells of my eyes
fringed with fern and pussy willow,
make saltwater taffy of my heart
sweet and soft and wax paper sealed
with the heated dew of your kisses.
I want beads of you braided all through my hair
want more than your rainbows –
something taboo.
I want your rain barrel arms — prodigious
and paddle boat legs — cypress from the bayou.
Give me
a long monsoon of you.

The Night Gardener
(from the Night Fairytales series)

The Night Gardener
deals with moths instead of bees
tends beds of ghosts instead of flowers
their pale all silver trumpets
shaking on the breeze.

The crop rows he walks
that 'reach as high as an elephant's eye'
are not stalks of corn that touch the sky
but stalks of dreams that stir and sigh.

He weeds them carefully,
plants by the light and the dark of the moon.
Bats and moles are birds out of tune
but he loves their peculiarities.

The Night Gardener I have heard it told
seeks not for fame, nor power, nor gold.
The only thing he wishes to receive in pay
is a bouquet of shooting stars to lay
in your arms on one night of the year.

Les Jours de Pluie

The days came gift wrapped
in ribbons of rain.
We ran our hands over the shimmer
of their outer wrappers as they melted
like sugar.
I can taste them still.

In those days
a constellation of coincidences
lit my way
and even the heavens, it seems,
were showing me the way to you.
I have memorized the path
without trying to.

When the sun rose,
when the rain stopped,
and I made my way blinking
from the tent of your arms
the birdsong soared
but not as high as my heart.
What use have I for this feather

that I saved? What use the memory
of sweetness
and a path that pulls me still
to want to wander?
Your arms have transformed
from woven tent to a stone wall
that I know not to loiter near.

the moon sets the scene

gilds the lily of your face
with special-effects-contact-lenses blue
I string an antler's worth
(tines in velvet moonlit too)
of kisses 'round your neck
no one can see them
but you feel them
I know that you do
you feel my aubergine kisses
when the moon is blue

The Moon Says Come Sit By Me, I'll Tell You a Story

The stars say they'll sparkle and shine
but the wind in the trees is what moves me
to tremble all leaf-like and fine
is the rustle in the dark of the forest
and the music of wild things and vine
purrs and merrowrs and huffs clary sage,
birch tar, labdanum, and pine.
I saved you a seat, some starlight, some moonlight,
I captured the breeze in my hair. The night is like wine
I've opened the bottle while I wait for you here.

I Am Thumbelina

I am Thumbelina in a field of flowers as tall as trees
gliding among the shadows of clouds of immensity
because everything is larger than life – when you walk with me.
Song starts on a subatomic level, twines itself to beat
like hammers made of hummingbirds
because even the minutest of things sing – when I am with you
and the greens chant and the sky is a sea to float away on a deux
as we lay in a field with Brobdingnagian flowers facing an ocean of blue.

he was helpless

her lashes swept slowly down
like willow trees bending
over the twin pools of her eyes
their tips wet
her tears sparkled –
a calligraphy of woe
curling serpentine but beautiful
as they curved down her face
past lips, an island bursting profusely
with roses, with orchids, with bougainvillea
and down to her chin which quivered just a little
just enough to shake those tears off
to land in his hand, holding her chin
and her tears, they disappeared into the cup
of his palm, sank their teeth into the very fiber of him
bit and pierced his heart
such was the power of her tears
over the fiercest warrior in the kingdom

She used to hate it

when they worked for the same company
and she could hear him coming down the hall
his voice rolling, low and gravelly, like thunder before him
arrested her hands at her keyboard
and wouldn't you know it
breath held for the stormy cocktail
of testosterone and pheromones to pass
she was left in his wake
soaked with a butterfly storm's worth of perspiration
dotting her upper lip
and trickling down her spine.
Nothing like perspiration stains first thing in the morning
at work,
am I right?

Golem Moon

The moon climbed up five floors.
There was no ivy, no rusty fire escape,
no Rapunzel tresses,
so the moon used bricks and shadows
to reach my windowsill
and brush aside the salt I poured as barrier.
The moon carried me down in his arms
and handed me to you.
Who knew he could be put to such golem tasks
to fetch and carry for you?
And I lay in your arms the whole night through
with your windows open wide
with the moon for a lamp that swayed in the wind
while I dreamt of the color blue.

I Wear My Heart Upon My Sleeve

I wear my heart upon my sleeve
And pinned there handsomely
By an heirloom brooch of ancient provenance
That was left to me.
And you can have both heart and brooch
As well as all of me
Just so long as you have managed
To bring with you the key.

The Fainting Couch of His Arms

She swooned into the fainting couch of his arms
and held her breath when smelling salts were offered.
No sir, no pungent remedy needed.
She was fine right there.

The moon hung around

outside my window all night
and worse than the brightness
(so I couldn't sleep)
and worse than the breeze
scented with dew
was the discourteous way
that the moon just kept talking
all night long about you.

"On Nights Like These," He Said

"When raindrops shiver on every tree
when the storm is a veil
covering the face of the sky
and thunder is the low drumbeat
of the heart of the night,
on every night but especially
on nights like these,
I want to pierce your mysteries."

Trees Sway Behind Your Eyes
(with a nod to Keats)

Trees sway behind your eyes.
Each green leaf turns its face up towards the sky
in the hopes of rain.
There is a storm within my heart
that was written with your name
and though your name 'be writ with water'
that storm is just the start
of the way that you are part of me
from roots to stormed tree-tops.

In Which Deep Blue Waves of Fabric Are Like the Famed Red Sea

Deep velvet skirts of blue
part like a sea
as if directed by a god's hand
to reveal the path of her thighs
covered in sheen lace
a salt licked land, a miracle,
that leads to a promised shore.
Can you get to the other side?

Untitled

droplets of sweat lick
the angles of your face, trace
their salty fingers

down your chest, make me want to
be the breeze that goose-bumps you

Painting the Leaves With Rain

The day paints the leaves with rain.
I want to wear the raindrops like jewelry:
like earrings the prisms of which slide against your lips
as you kiss my rain slicked neck,
like a necklace that wraps around us both
lassoing us into thickets of storm
that we are glad to lose ourselves within.

To-do List

Did you miss the sun this morning
as he walked the dogs of heaven
and whistled the light into the sky?
He made breakfast for the moon
but when he brought it to her,
she was no longer in his bed.
On his to-do list today:
1. Spread light to all the world.
2. Do a little nuclear fusion.
3. Then talk to Moon, persuade her
to always wake in his bed — and to stay for breakfast too.

Still

The traffic of your regard
still crosses the bridge of my senses
not pedestrian, not vehicular,
but something with hooves –
a wild horse runs bareback to my hand
still makes me want to gallop fast and hard.

A Love That Is Not Meant To Be

Fire trucks wail
and our cat is sure their siren song
is just for her
a love song and a ululation of desire.
There is no dissuading her
from her posture of anticipation
trembling on the "balcony" (the windowsill)
in wait for Romeo.

Riders On the Rain

Under the wind's translucent sheets
diamonds fall,
raindrops sharp as knives and cold as steel,
but they don't touch me.
It is as if there is a space of grace around me.
I am a sigh, a feather touch
against your black back
but you still feel me
through the leather of your jacket
and my hair, Medusa ribbons,
winds itself like a scarf of silk
streaming in the wind.

A Cold Morning

Frost rides the pale blue horse of sky
that comes galloping through the dark woods of my dreams.
The birds take to the air to trail in long reins of song.
My heart is the grass, green and glad in its clover
beneath the mounting dawn.

Haiku

I sit in the arms
of dilapidated couch
wish those arms were yours

The Wind In the Trees

The breeze runs its fingers through the trees
like a lover's touch through tangled hair,
whispers secrets to the leaves
that I can't help but overhear.

By the water of the lake I wait –
the fish beneath the satin sheets of water
can hear the beating of my heart
as can the frogs and birds, the foxes and the deer

that nibble at the shoots along the shore.
On nights like this longing is a kite
pulled by the string of our desire.
I close my eyes and lean into the wind.

the moonlight

falls like white ribbons through the dark
ties the trees up like presents and curls
along the ground in shades of blue
twists in such a way that makes me want
to see you wrapped in moonbeams too

"Can I?"

"Can I have all your rainy days?" she asked.
"And all my rainy nights too." he agreed,
not knowing she was a weather mage
and that he was in for some stormy weather indeed.

"Can I have all your kisses?" she asked.
"Yes, you can have all my kisses and all my smiles besides."
he said,
and she smiled little knowing he was a master mage
whose kisses were his magic, whose smiles were just like
wine.

Sunday Things: Green Rocks, Red Ones, and White Ones

You give me green rocks.
You call them jade, say they are money.
I say “Illusion”, let them slip fast like shadows
through my fingers spread wide.

You give me red rocks.
You call them rubies, say they are passion.
I say “Concupiscence” as they sizzle and slide,
trail scorch marks out of my hands.

You give me white rocks.
You call them diamonds, say they are beauty.
I say “Avarice” as I cast them on water
I see them flash as I throw them aside.

You give me no rocks
come empty handed
ask what I want, say “Tell me what kind”.
“This is love,” I say
as I take your empty hands
and I fill them with mine.

my right ear

is a chocolate box
filled with your sweet confections
even the moon leans in closer
hoping to overhear

The river of night

laps at the shore
of my wakefulness.
I walk boulevards lined with lamp post stars
and catch the lamp lighter's song on my lips.
Before I know it
wavelets lick at my bare feet
toenails painted black to match the sky
and this dark velvet's indigo dye.
I am drawn towards the moon
at the end of the lane
left like a lover's lamp
to light my way to you.

Pieces of Sky

The trees crowd one another
trying to be the first
to give bouquets
of fresh green leaves
to the warm air.

Looking through
their gift-filled hands
I want to slip through
their fingers
and pluck
pieces of sky –
(an ethereal type
of spring harbinger
blooming in shades of blue)

bring fat roses
(azure, robins egg, Tiffany, true)
home for my table, to scent the air
to wear in my hair...
and to wrap in a nosegay for you.

Plate Spinner

You are not the kind of guy
who likes to eat off one plate
no matter how fine the shine
delicate the bone china
or inscrutable the design.
You want the whole china cabinet
the plates, large dinner and small dessert
the bowls and cups and saucers too
even the gravy boat are taken out and used.

You are a plate spinner
and a tablecloth trick sinner.

I am just determined
not to be one of those sparkling pieces
of porcelain
spinning dizzily like crazy
and destined for the floor.

Smoke on the air

Let the past be
like smoke on the air
just a trace of proof
that there ever was
such a great blaze
between you and me
that set whole forests on fire
set the world on fire too
with flames licking the ceiling of the sky
curling the painted clouds off
and even managing to steam the cold stars
to unusual brilliance.

Let the past dissipate
while it drifts its way backwards
and becomes harder and harder to see.

Thickets

You bring me words
sweet and succulent
hold them in the hands of your mind –
hands scratched by thorns
and with dirt beneath their nails.

Your mouth is a basket overflowing
with hand-picked berries just for me.
Your eyes show me flashes
of fur, of feathers
in the thickets of your thoughts.
Vines cover every branch
in sinuous, sensuous green.

You want me
to walk with you
in the wild wood.
I want those berries
your thorn-scratched hands
and your basket too.

Braille, Script, Codex

I wish to learn your hard muscles
and sculpted lines like I am blind
to everything but the Braille of your skin
that rises to kiss my fingertips,
a script written in desire,
each rope of muscle a codex
for my curiosity to explore
all the while the wild tale of you
catches my breath and hammers my
heart –
percussive exclamation points
punctuate your beautiful font
and leave me breathless for more.

White Snow and Bad Girl Boots *(slow melt)*

As the temperature rises
there is a slow striptease removal
of white lacy things.

Streams and inlets swell
rivulets roll dreamily
as the snow melts in a long sigh

breathes softly against the stiff wind
and all the while Winter wears
her thigh-high boots.

She won't take them off
till Spring comes.

Standing Tall

Your glances walk tingles
right up the ladder of my spine.
My posture wears high heels
(hips tilted and shoulders thrust back)
even in my bare feet
when I run into the hydraulic lift
of your eyes.

Day Longs for Night

The night
lets down her long dark gypsy hair
spins on her bare feet
and stomps her passion
for moths, black blooms
bats and all things witchy.

The moonlight,
her Mona Lisa smile,
mysterious and subtle, suffuses her
wild beauty
with a gentleness so fragile
it can be broken by
the ephemera of clouds.

Pieces of her hair
catch in the swaying trees
to curl and dry by morning's light
into Spanish moss
as if the trees
could not bear
to let her go.

And she had no princess slipper
to leave upon the lawn
but she left dewdrops
crystal beads of perspiration
for day to come upon.

Day spends his time plotting
ways to find her in his arms –
the sunset a prayer, a beacon,
a campfire, for her wandering to find.

The black oyster of night

is open wide
showing the hard pearl of the moon
like a ring in a velvet lined box.

A Modern Day Persephone

I slip my feet into high heels
that strut me through my day
four inches of stiletto steel
that leave exclamation points
instead of flowers

springing like arrows of desire
everywhere my heel has pressed

like a lover's kiss to the waiting
ready, wanting, ground...

The Cliché of Cherry-Stained-Lips

He says:
When you are near
nothing comes to mind
but cherry-stained-lips and sky-blue-eyes.
And even in my thoughts these clichés
clang together like empty cans
to crush against my inner forehead
like the Neanderthal guy
that you bring out in me
all Caliban lack of grace.

She says:
Don't underestimate
the appeal that a hairy knuckle
bent with gentleness can bring
or the way your confusion
can cause my heart to swing.
That forehead crushed can
has left its dent along your inner skin
and I am strangely drawn
to mark it with a kiss.

Tanka

Dandelion fluff
snows against hot summer panes
delicate flurries.
Unbanked, memories of you
thaw, rushing melt of longing.

White Veils and Fire

I see down-filled counterpanes
spilling on the air
hear the whisper of wool
feel the kiss of cashmere
and the static crackle of polyester
in this storm.

The snow swirls sequins-and-glitter feet
that do not want to touch the ground
and Salome dances
with white veils tonight.

The spectacle makes me want
you
to cover me
wrap around me
all through the night
be my blanket
keep me warm and
hold me tight.

Just because Salome
is mentioned in this poem
there is no need to think
of John the Baptist
and his head served up
Martha Stewart style
to pay for others' concupiscence.

Let any thought of baptisms be limited to
that of skin against skin
and the baptism of fire
between we two.

Tanka

Perigean tides –
I am oceans and wild seas.
You are the full moon.
Tides rise and banks are flooded –
to the pull and sway of you

Falling
(from The Consequence of Wings)

Falling in love with you
is like throwing myself
into the arms of the night
and I am afraid
of the dark
unknown.

But there is the promise
of moonlight
and trees and grasses stirred
by your breeze.
There are white pillows
fat with dreams

and the thought that when you turn
your face to me at last
it will be morning that looks at me
with nighttime's promise behind the blinds
of your almond shaped eyes.

Oh what's the rush?
(from The Consequence of Wings)

I guess you think
if you don't cage the bird
that it will fly away

take its soft throat
Valkyrie winds
somewhere
you can't follow.

Don't you know
that birds love you
and that flight and heaven
mean nothing
without you?

A Fairy Tale Come True
(from The Real Reason the Queen Hated Snow)

(Pipe)
You, the Pied Piper of Hamlin
to my words, lure, entice.
They come, the children of my thoughts
running-tumbling-skipping at your call
dash through the heavily guarded portcullis
of my mouth
and just like in the story
they are gone–I can't take them back.

(Prick)
I pricked my finger
on the spindle of your tongue
and now my common sense is heavy lidded
my intuition sleeps.
All the while, breadcrumbs are being pecked
by birds with pin-top shiny eyes
and a ball of twine recoils upon itself.

(Snap!)
Here's another story:
My gingerbread heart
ran and ran and ran singing
"You can't catch me. Nobody can."
The clever fox of your hands
promised to carry it to safety–
holds it still
in glad-handed jaw grip.

sweet summer day

latticework leaves tendril the sky
casting shadows
like the sly half-mast of lashes
curled against the soft cheek of the grass

the brook arches an eyebrow
and slips its arms around the whole scene
whispering to the woods and the field to come away
come away, on a sweet summer day

With Birds

You are the seashell I put to my ear
to hear the roar of seas
I have never seen.
Your voice is the wind winding through
pearl chambers and pushing
the tide like an unsaid wish into my ear–
salt rims and bird cries echo
the rise and fall.

Wind Chimes
Your words are beads
and shiny pieces of metal
and glass and feathers
strung upon strings
in my window
for the breeze of your voice
to move through–
and they chime–
they chime and they scare away ghosts;
they sing like many colored birds in summer trees.

Storm
Your voice is a storm
that I run out into
to get wind tossed and soaked by the rain;
hitch a ride on a passing farmhouse,
search all the cupboards and closets
for fortuitous besom
and fling myself confidently from the window
and onto the air
that is filled with birds.

Tree
And when I come down
I root myself and grow, become a tree
just to have you whisper your secrets
through my leaves
just to have you snake through my limbs

sway my always reaching higher for the sky...
and you bring me birds, again, as presents.
I wear them on my branches
like multicolored rings
and the song of you rocks me to my roots.

Winter Things

You think of cold and ice
bare branches and black skies
tracks that get lost in the snow.

I think of stars to find my way by
flames that lick the night away
the softness of your skin, of your fur,
of your sighs.

I will help you dig
so that we can
burrow in together
for the winter season.

You will bring me branches
of ice, as beautiful as diamonds
which will melt
but I will have had them
for a while

and when the snow has melted
all paths will lead to the river
but you won't see me there.

Look to the sky and the horizon
I will be wearing wings,
the ones you gave me
and I will take you with me.

Green Eyes Flecked With Gold

Green grasses stir behind your eyes.
All the flowers in the grasses purr
like golden cats
like tiny suns
maned with honeybees
that are busy making me lose myself
in those green grasses flecked with gold.
They are buzzy making me want to
lie down in your fields and just breathe
in the perfume that sighs upon the air there,
in the place behind/within your eyes,
the vistas of your soul.

I Knew a Man *(to be read in a Southern voice)*

I knew a man.
I knew a man who
when the crisp crunch of win in his hand
was replaced
with the soft Play-Doh squeeze of nothing
rubbed his hands together
and made a snake
out of that Play-Doh nothing
and sent that snake on a snake's favorite errand
that of tempting an Eve.
I knew a man pretended his nothing
had a hood as stand-up as a cobra's.
His hands were closed
so it couldn't be seen
that they were empty indeed.
Not only did I know him,
that snake charming man,
but the Eve in the story was me.
So, when his snake done rolled up on me
I gave it my heel
and planted my own sin's-delight-tree.

The Golden Bough

(from The Real Reason the Queen Hated Snow)

"I beheld fate looming for Balder,
Wooden's son,
the bloody victim."

If it's true that I took my soul
and put it into an external object
for cherishing and safekeeping,
it is also true that this protection
has grown tusked
bars, has kept me half alive
and never free.

"There stands the mistletoe
slender and delicate,
blooming high above the ground."

In Winter, mistletoe stays green
against the leafless oak
and grows not from the ground
but perches, like a verdant soul
upon the branches of the tree.

"Hod shall shoot it, but Friga
in Fen-hall, shall weep over
the woe of Wal-hall."

The very sprig of my vitality
blindly (is love always blind?)
let loose against me
unstrings my heart
which crumbles golden
like withered mistletoe.

And mistletoe is ever harvested
in this way, situated between heaven

and earth, never allowed to touch the ground
but cut by pith scythe and caught on white cloth.

Weave for me a crown of thorns,
green flowers, white berries, cloven
from the golden bough that grows
on soul's-desire tree–
weep amber tears and kiss
in remembrance of me.

Your voice pours over me

Like honey
Slow, sweet and sticky
Makes every word you say stick
To me like feathers
I wear a plumage of your expressions
Tarred and feathered but the tar is golden honey
And the feathers fletched from you.

A bright splinter of her spirit will

pierce your heart and be with you always.
It will hurt and comfort at the same time
and will shine so brightly
that you can see it in the dark with your eyes closed.
When you place your hand over this gift/wound
it will come away cupping light.

Petal Soft and Candy Sweet

The clouds are petals of softness
a lavish trail that scents the sky
with promises
of summer.
You touch me
and I feel the rise and swell
of stamen
yearn towards the butterfly –
flower power –
I blush
crimson
and
flush
though I'm no clinging
wallflower.
I am wild honeysuckle.
A drop of nectar
falls
and I lick it off
my bee stung lips,
my velvet tilting
and my heavy nodding head
measures the stiff breeze
that mounts the grass
which presses its mouth
against your back
beneath me.
You make me blossom
everywhere you touch.
Such flowers kindle
candy
for my memory
to suck.
I'll take each piece
from its fancy sleeve
of scalloped white

and breathe deep
the spring morning
that clings like melted chocolate
from their touch.

You call me Angel

talk about the covenant of my eyes
the harp of my lips.

I want you
to see that if I am an angel
I am fallen.

My face is in shadow to you
who are blinded by the halo
of your 'perceptions'
so how can you even know me?

My heel is round, rosily angelic
but tapers to pointed toes
cloven cantered
striking sparks on many-colored stones
and I could easily be the Queen of Tyre.

Will you braid me a Jacob's ladder?
Will you douse a flaming sword?
Will you pledge white robes
and give
the weightlessness of feathers
something to cleave to?

They came out of nowhere

with stealth and stingers
pierced me
and left
two stings for me
a gift in a way -- a mnemonic device.
I can truly say of those two wasps that materialized (like
magic!)
out of the green and beautiful hedge, that the way they left
me
with heat beneath my skin --
an itch and a pain combined
in a swollen blush --
puts me in mind of both times I was stung
by the bite of love for you.
Wasps are assholes.

Salamander Song

I was his chameleon
shimmer skinned and ever changing
reminding him of all the best parts
of his former lovers.
But he never saw
the part that was only me.
And my stories
my salamander songs
from the heart of the fire
of creativity
distracted him
for a while.
But he never heard
my words like waves
crashing on the shore
of my soul's sea.
Sea song and fire hiss
both belong to me
but he never saw it coming
that I was leaving.
He was blinded by the surface shine
and lost to the depths of me.

www.ingramcontent.com/pod-product-compliance
Lightning Source LLC
Chambersburg PA
CBHW071103090426
42737CB00013B/2461

9780692581162